The Poet's Domain

The Poet's Domain

Collections of Poems
by Writers in Maryland, Virginia
and the District of Columbia

Volume Six
Nets To Catch the Wind

Compiled and Edited by
Joseph D. Adams

"Books Worth Your Time"
Box 172 • Fairfax Station, Va. 22039

Copyright © 1992 by ROAD Publishers

All rights reserved
including the right of reproduction
in whole or in part in any form.

Published by
ROAD Publishers
Box 172
Fairfax Station, Va. 22039

Designed by Donna L. Robinson

ISBN 1-880016-10-9 **6.95**

Printed in the United States of America

CONTENTS

                    A Note from the Publisher xi
                           The Editor's Preface xii

Barbara H. Achilles, Vienna, Va.
                                     Choices 1
                            f-8 and Be There 2
      When Lilacs Now in the Graveyard Grow 3

Patricia Adler, Woodbridge, Va.
                                  Couplets 4

M. Ray Allen, Clifton Forge, Va.
                  Near Graduation from Radford 5

Joseph Awad, Richmond, Va.
                      Notebook Entry, October 7
   The Young Poet Voices His Love for the City 7
                                  California 8

Lolete Falck Barlow, Camp Springs, Md.
                              Still Waters 9
                                Convictus 9

Mary Kay Belter, Vienna, Va.
                         Motor Cycle Rose 10
                              Meditation 11
                               Interaction 11

Patsy Anne Bickerstaff, Weyers Cave, Va.
                                 Heirloom 12
                                         Haze 13

Sheila Cardano, Cape Charles, Va.
Watching the Sunset   14

Kathy L. Cawthon, Hampton, Va.
The Battle   15

Eunice de Chazeau, Alexandria, Va.
John Gardner O   16
Artemesia   17

J.P.Q. El-Fayoumy, Virginia Beach, Va.
Winter Street, Cape Cod, 1941   18

Laddie Fisher, Roanoke, Va.
Night is Gone   19

Linda Beth Fristoe, Front Royal, Va.
La Lune D'Hiver Sur Mes Seines   20
Midnight Monologue   21
With You   21
Endymion's Embrace   22

Gertrude Gunther, Onancock, Va.
Partridgeberry   23
Common Mullein, Icon   23
"The Coffee's Cold." "It Always Is."   24

Ann Hawes, Alexandria, Va.
The Small Person   25

Barbara McKay Hewin, Williamsburg, Va.
Gray   26
April Rain   26

Alana Maubury Hunter, Arlington, Va.
Trained To Shoot Off   27
Glimpse   27

Agnes Nasmith Johnston, Alexandria, Va.
Valley of Grief   28
Brush Strokes   28
Refugees   29

Carrie Jackson Karegeannes, Annandale, Va.
    Dupont Circle   30
    More Than Music   30

Jean P. Klotzbach, Columbia, Md.
    By the Opera House   31
    The Wind   31

Olive S. Lanham, Daytona Beach, Fla.
    March Moon   32
    Winter Menu   32

Mary Antil Lederman, Charlottesville, Va.
    Parlor Talk   33
    China in Mourning   34
    Holding Tight ... With Open Arms ...   34

John Long, Richmond, Va.
    Tree Dreaming   35
    The Glad Insomniac   36
    Geographic   37

Michael Hugh Lythgoe, Gainesville, Va.
    Nets   38
    Ballad for Forsythia   39
    Long Key   40

Barbara Mabe, Wake, Va.
    A Boy's God   41

Joan Maloof, Quantico, Md.
    Breathing with Daddy   42

Dorothy W. Millner, Alexandria, Va.
    Island Therapy   43
    Time's Fool   43

Medea E. Minnich, Ijamsville, Md.
    Encounter at the Agri-Service   44

Robert R. Montgomery, Hartfield, Va.
    Incarnation   45

Geneva Ingraham Nasworthy, Woodstock, Va.
Chalice Holder 46
Tiger 46

Julie Vakos Nordstrom, Exmore, Va.
Birth 48
City Scene 48

Daisy Oblinger, Madison Heights, Va.
Lord of the Harvest 49

David J. Partie, Lynchburg, Va.
Looking for Pebbles on Moonstone Beach 50
The Whiteness of the Page 51

Jennifer Peachey, Bristol, Va.
The Autistic Child 52

Richard Raymond, III, Midlothian, Va.
Cradle Song 53

Evelyn Ritchie, Richmond, Va.
Hero of Richmond Theatre Fire, 1811 54
"I Myself and No Other" 55
The Giver 56

Ada G. Sanderson, Falls Church, Va.
Thoreau's Walk in Winter 57

Askold Skalsky, Ijamsville, Md.
Love's Platform 58
Taking Stock 58

Barbara Smith, Newport News, Va.
Hebrew Class 59

Bruce Souders, Winchester, Va.
Plea for an Oracle 60
Under Spring Skies 60
Early Summer: An Alpine Epiphany 61

Isobel Routly Stewart, Woodbridge, Va.
Highway Interchange 62

Constance Tupper, Charlottesville, Va.
  Babushka 63
  Aunt Josie 63

Adrian Robert Unger, Radford, Va.
  Where Are the Fairy Tales? 64

Evelyn Amuedo Wade, Alexandria, Va.
  Two of a Kind—My Cat and Me 65

Susannah A. Warner, Onancock, Va.
  Henbit and Winter Wheat 66

Sharon Weinstein, Virginia Beach, Va.
  Daughter's Breaks 67
  Spring 67
  Men Touching 68
  Sabbath Morning 68
  Dying 68

Katherine Roberts Wescott, Onancock, Va.
  Windjammer 70
  Really-rilly 71

Moraeg E. Wood, Charlottesville, Va.
  Thought 72

Deborah Woodward, Richmond, Va.
  Chase 73

Dorothy Yeatman, Salisbury, Md.
  Classic Courtship 74
  One Poet's Passions 75
  Tidewater 76

Israel Zoberman, Virginia Beach, Va.
  At Maidanek 77
  I Longingly 77
  There is a Sadness 77

ALPHABETICAL INDEX OF POETS 79

A Note from the Publisher

The Poet's Domain is ROAD Publishers' series of collected contemporary poetry by writers in or from Virginia, Maryland, and the District of Columbia.

We proudly publish these special poetry collections in limited edition volumes. In addition to demonstrating that good poets are actively at work in Virginia, Maryland, and the District of Columbia (and with volume seven, the state of Delaware), these books provide the quality showcase these fine poets deserve.

To keep poetry accessible to readers, ROAD Publishers offers these volumes at modest prices without sacrificing quality of production.

To date the works of more than one hundred poets have appeared in *The Poet's Domain*. Future volumes to will display greater numbers of quality works by greater numbers of fine regional poets. Key biographical information about the poets acquaints readers with the poets.

In the present volume, the poets address a number of concerns. They want to engage readers. Readers, in turn, may engage them through us.

Donna L. Robinson
Publisher

The Editor's Preface

For the sixth volume of *The Poet's Domain*, we take our title, *Nets To Catch the Wind*, from John Webster (1580-1625). His *The Devil's Law Case*, written in 1623, a time when political dissent was on the rise, spurred on by religious unrest (the ascendancy of Calvinistic thinking and a violent anti-catholic backlash), contains these lines:

> Vain the ambition of kings
> Who seek by trophies and dead things
> To leave a living name behind,
> And weave but *nets to catch the wind*.

The lines link the folly of secular aspirations and desires to the empty enterprises of aristocratic rulers and supply us a shrewd metaphor for activities that have neither valid purpose nor fruitful result.

Poets have perennially mused upon human folly, which ranges from stupidity and idiocy to imprudence or indiscretion, foolish schemes present in every society at every age, poetically expressed as "nets to catch the wind". The obverse, of course, is the human yearning for consideration, for good will, for sane and reasonable conduct, all of which restores order to our chaotic world.

When we proposed *Nets To Catch the Wind*, regional poets responded in record number. From the poems submitted, we selected ninety-seven that offered varied and provocative viewpoints on empty enterprises, many of them startling.

We hasten to reveal certain editorial predispositions that may give rise to suspicions of misdirection. The viewpoints expressed on some subjects in certain poems must be viewed in several ways: first, a poet may assert directly that the action of the poem is indeed an empty enterprise. If that action seems absurd to us as readers, we readily accept the poet's estimate of the situation. However, if that action seems reasonable to us, we may question the poet's judgment.

That takes us to a second reading: the poet may assert the flip side of the empty enterprise, its antithesis. Folly and sense form a dichotomy, two sides of the same issue, like hot and cold, sweet and sour, pleasure and pain. As readers, we must look for clues that reveal to us how the poet really stands on the issue.

And that takes us to our third reading: the poet may present an ironical view of a human belief or activity in the hope that we will recognize the mocking intent of the satirical portrayal. In any case, the poet gets off scot free. The reader, as usual, must be astute. *Caveat emptor.*

Joseph D. Adams
Painter, Virginia
August 1992

The best place to meet
the poets of the region
is in
THE POET'S DOMAIN

Barbara H. Achilles

Choices

I prefer old mountains. Democratic,
Gentle slopes shaped by eons of
    unending elements.
Accessible to all.

Elitist Everest, I eschew.
I leave it to the favored few
Because it's there.

For me, no frantic, scrambling, clawing
    climb
Up a jagged, jutting presence: a pop-up
    peak
Lately thrust into our midst;
An afterthought appended to the planet
By some itinerant architect.

For me, no dodging through volcanic
    landscapes
Littered with lava and debris, ejected
In some cosmic case of indigestion.

I set my sights
On modest heights.

An easy day's meandering journey
To reach a summit at vesper time
To commune with Olympians of like
    mind
And share the golden vision of
A fresh Allegheny spring,
A cool Adirondack summer,
A rich Appalachian fall.

No wild, international acclaim
When I have reached my goal.
Only a quiet celebration in my soul.

The view is no less grand,
Nor effort less rewarding
Than from a mighty Alp—
Just different.

Barbara H. Achilles (b. 1931, Knowlesville, NY), a former music director, scriptwriter, and intelligence officer, graduated from the Eastman School of Music and the College of Arts and Sciences, University of Rochester. Since her poetry debut in *The Poet's Domain*, Vol. 5, she has had poetry accepted for publication in *The Wall Street Journal* and has received prizes in the Poetry Society of Virginia annual competition. A resident of Vienna, VA, she is currently working on a collection of profiles of minor historical figures.

Barbara H. Achilles

f-8 and Be There

Formidable fine arts photographer,
Nikon and Hasselblad strapped to his chest.
Vest pockets bulging with lenses and filters.
Carpe Dawn! Carpe Dusk!
Never shoots from ten to three—
Mid-day light not worthy of his lens.
He measures.
He meters.
Composes the scene.
Saw that limb!
Move those wires!
Stop that traffic!
Days of labor;
Thousands of dollars;
Miles of film.
In the end,
Another fine landscape captured.

Businessman Abraham Zapruder,
Occasional home movie buff,
At noon on a bright November day
Brings his old Bell and Howell 8 mm
To Dealey Plaza
Just in time
To shoot the shots seen round the world.

Barbara H. Achilles

When Lilacs Now in the Graveyard Grow

I finally found John,
his marker hidden by a luxuriant
    growth of lilacs;
a living memorial planted by some
    well-meaning mourner.

Oldest son? Not really.
He bore the family name even though
he was the product of his mother's
    youthful indiscretion.

Father of four? Not really.
Who knows how many more he
    spawned
in years of illicit liaisons and casual
    encounters.

Pillar of the community? Not really.
His accomplishments were legend.
    Mythological
would be more accurate; a creation of
    admiring peers.

The lilac bush grows larger with each
    passing year,
obscuring the real measure of the man
    and
the small marker that is truly his.

Patricia Adler

Couplets

I love you, more than anything else.
I love you too. We're forever.

I love you, we're just right together.
I love you too, please don't ever leave me.

I love you.
I love you too.

Do you still love me?
Of course I do.

I don't think you love me anymore.
I wouldn't be here if I didn't.

I still love you.
...

I'm going to a therapist.
Don't think I'm going.

Are we going to work on our relationship or what?
Don't give me ultimatums.

I think we've plateau'd.
You're my best friend.

I need a lover.
I do too—but I want you.

It looks like we've grown old together.
It wasn't easy.

Would you do it again?
Yes.

Patricia Adler (b. 1938, Elizabeth, NJ), a teacher for 20 years, presently works as a secretary. She makes her poetry debut in this edition. She lives in Woodbridge and is currently studying commercial and graphic art at Northern Virginia Community College.

M. Ray Allen

Near Graduation from Radford

Working eleven to seven at the 7-Eleven,
James pulls forty hours a week
while most of his college classmates
    sleep.
Making another pot of coffee,
he sees in grounds the nests of weaver
    birds
turn dark ornaments in eucalyptus
    branches
framed stark by horizon sun.
Entering the Rift Valley again,
he sees gazelle flash beyond ant hills
higher than the shelves he stacks,
sees elephants bookend their young
beside the water hole
as pride of lions approaches
and Kilimanjaro wedges whiter into the
    sky
than the ice he pours into the cup
to make another slurpee.
Sweeping the parking lot near daybreak,
he sees giraffe browsing on the veldt
beyond the limb where the leopard
    sleeps
with front paws dangling,
sees rhinos charge the sounds of things
their squinting eyes cannot make out.
Hitchhiking across town,
he yearns for the rough ride
from Nairobi to the Rift again
where the lion drags the wildebeest
toward shade of acacia and waiting
    mate.
Walking by the New River,
mud cakes spread like a jigsaw puzzle,
and he sees the beetle pull itself
from eye socket of zebra
and crawl past clean-picked rib cage
that curves its shadow on parched earth
to form the only stripes that are left.
In the river's slow green flow,
his reflection calls to him

M. Ray Allen (b. 1941, Martin, KY), a poet, playwright, and journalist, has won more than twenty poetry awards since making his debut as a poet at the opening ceremony for the Douglass House Center in Long Beach, CA, in 1968. The author of *The Roads I Travel* (Nightshade Press, 1990) and *Between the Thorns: Windcarver Songs of Appalachia* (ROAD Publishers, 1991), he was inducted into the Morehead State University Alumni Hall of Fame in 1991.

M. Ray Allen

from distant waters whispering
in Swahili: Truth without deceit,
your own *North Star* awaits you
for soon is the time for returning.

Joseph Awad

Notebook Entry, October

I stand in a golden sunshine
(I like its heat on my neck and back)
While a rush of wind flails the leaves
Of the lush red maple. I stay to watch
Their shuffling shadows do-si-do
With sunlight dancing on the grass.
I make these lines lest a lovely moment
Be lost forever when I pass.

The Young Poet Voices His Love for the City

What favors can you fashion for her?
What loot or lore, what splendor
Pour out at her feet?
How outdo the largest of those others,
Those other lovers?

Beguile her with bejeweled virelays,
With glittering rhymes, with opulent
    images
Of April's golden ambiguities.
Crush the *grappa* of a summer dusk
Into a bootleg burgundy of language
To purple her proud lips.
On windborne metaphors
Sweep like a caress
Across the silken kirtle of her lights,
And guess the deepest secrets of her
    nights.

And when she throws you over,
When you must lose her to those
    aftercomers,
Flash the switchblade of a streetsmart
    art.
Cut across her heart a singing scar.

Joseph Awad (b. 1929, Shenandoah, PA), who lives in Richmond, VA, is a vice-president of the Poetry Society of Virginia and was recently named to the Virginia Communications Hall of Fame. His poems have appeared in numerous journals and anthologies including previous volumes of *The Poet's Domain*. His books include *The Neon Distances* (Golden Quill Press, 1980), *Construction Ahead* (Sparrow Press, 1989) and *Shenandoah Long Ago* (The Poet's Press, 1990).

Joseph Awad

California

There is foreboding in the rumble
Of hidden faults, of ocean gnawing
Sunlit cliffs. Potted palms,
Relics of stardoms long foregone,
Droop in dark, art deco lobbies
Of old hotels in Hollywood. Haze
Hangs, a deepening premonition,
Over the freeways and the purple
    mountains
Of the angel Gabriel.

To this land of no pedestrians,
Of desert distances and dreams
Plummeting over jagged canyons,
Of lights in the night hills
And lights in the night valleys,
With whining tires leaving home behind
For miles of loneliness, we come
Like winds across the great divide,
Sifting in mountainous imaginations
The lost treasure of the Sierra Madre.

Lolete Falck Barlow

Still Waters

How little
   I ripple
      the waters of
         your life

You
   who created
      tidal waves
         in mine.

Sometimes
   when the moon is right
   I look at
      buoys

And wonder
   just how deep
   still waters
      run.

Convictus

Remember me no better than I am.
Nor worse! For I have faults enough,
   and more,
to keep me from the fellowship of saints.
And yet, I pray that neither will you
   damn
my lack of angel wings. The Editor
will judge me soon enough, and your
   complaints
are doubtless on His list. If my
   constraints
are greater than you wish, inheritor
of heaven I would be—provided good
intentions tip the scale. We can't ignore
the rules without a price; it's grievous
   sham
denying what the heart holds true. I
   could
but hope that time will prove you
   understood.
Apologies go on ad nauseam!

Lolete Falck Barlow (b. 1932, Mobile, AL) is the wife of a retired Air Force officer and mother of three. Her time is divided between their home in Camp Springs, MD, and "Bay View," their waterfront retreat in North Beach on Chesapeake Bay. Past president of the Alexandria Branch, National League of American Pen Women, her award winning poems have appeared in numerous periodicals. She's Poetry Editor of the Pen Woman magazine and, between home-improvement projects, is currently at work on a first book of poems.

Mary Kay Belter

Motor Cycle Rose

Studs, stars in a pool of night,
March down bull-hide armor
With shoved up sleeves.
A dragon, needled into skin, breaths fire
On muscle taunt as a spring.

His black cycle, rumbling
Like the engine of a battleship,
Defies all males;
Chrome flashes, "Try me, if you dare!"
He weaves through trucks,
Like a bull herding his harum.

He halts at the light;
I study his macho.
Black curls sneak from onyx helment,
Stubble shades his jaw,
A cigaret dangles from lips
Set like a crowbar,
His eyes bore through iron, stone.

When he turns
My breath is stunned into pause,
His jacket zipper, open,
Like a Freudian slip,
Reveals a dozen velvet-red roses,
Settled in floral wrap,
Stuffed down his t-shirt.

He smiles and winks.

Mary Kay Belter (b. 1948, Hobart, OK) studied biology at George Mason University and worked with the National Park Service for two years. Her work has appeared in *The Poet's Domain*, Vols. 2, 3, 4, and 5. She lives with her husband and two children in Vienna, VA.

Mary Kay Belter

Meditation

Words cease speaking;
In the astral, boundaries fade;
Shoulds, oughts lose their voices,
Heaving quiets into serene.
Time is suspended in passing.
I go inside, outside,
Walk naked into echoes,
Bump noses with the ohm inside.
I join kindred to reach into the quiet
Of a chime reverberating salty.
The hush after the last note
Draws us into its vortex.
We merge into the unwordable
That melds human into sea and stone,
Into azure, violet, and mauve.
Excitement,
Contained in a flask,
Opens, softens in anticipation,
Draws with webs spun by a spider tip
    toeing
Across the stars.

Interaction

He bellow-attacks.
She notices intent,
But returns soft curiosity,
Intense calm.
His fingers dart, like striking snakes
Around her wrist.
Flowing into his movement
She rides his energy,
Feels direction, power.
She blends into unity,
Diverts, redirects, rechannels,
Sweeps him into her circling,
Deposits him on the ground.
Looking up, he attempts
To reconstruct his landing at her feet.
He arises with returning anger
To attack again.
Once more her movement flows,
Harmonizes,
Draws his into hers,
And he falls at her feet.
He rises, shrugs,
And saunters away.

Patsy Anne Bickerstaff (b. 1940, Richmond, VA) has degrees in English and Law from the University of Richmond. An officer in the Poetry Society of Virginia, and a member of the Virginia Writers' Club, she is listed in *Writers in Virginia* and *Poets & Writers*. Her work has appeared in over fifty publications, including Vol. 1 of *The Poet's Domain*. She lives in Weyers Cave with her husband, novelist Wilson Lee Seay.

Patsy Anne Bickerstaff

Heirloom

In the folds of Dickenson County hills,
in a coal-vein town, on a Saturday night,
when the mines were closed, supper
    dishes cleared,
and Sunday shirts hung by the door,
with soot-dust washed from face and
    hair,
Uncle Zeb used to play his mandolin
by the kerosene lamp in our wide front
    room,
and my granddaddy joined him by and
    by,
with a fiddle that sang in his big hard
    hands.
They would start from a tune so sad
    and old,
no one alive could remember its name.
They would follow it up with
    "Wildwood Flower,"
or with "Sally Goodin" or "Salty Dog";
the men would sip from a Mason jar
that somebody brought from
    who-knows-where.
Then my granddaddy's fiddle rang high
    and sweet
with notes of "Bile Dem Cabbage
    Down";
we clapped while Grandma Miranda
    clogged,
tapping steps that she learned from her
    Grandpa Sean,
who had sailed from Limerick, long ago,
with the shirt on his back and his jigs
    and reels.
In her hard-soled shoes, on the bare
    wood floor,
she could dance like a gypsy queen
with a step as light as a leprechaun's;
she could dance like a bride of
    twenty-one
whose green eyes laughed with brand
    new dreams.
She could dance like the wind in a
    sumac tree,

Patsy Anne Bickerstaff

till her pinned-up ribbons of shining hair
fell and bounced on her shoulders like silver toys.
Her feet would flash in the lamplight's glow;
she could dance, she could dance, she could dance all night.

She lay at last in the same front room,
in her wedding gown, her green eyes still,
and the kitchen stacked with raisin pies.
No one saw two pigtail girls
who slipped out back to the smokehouse door.
In the hickory smell and wall-crack light,
I stood beside my cousin June
with solemn lips and big wet eyes,
and we practiced steps that our grandma danced.

Haze

Long-winged, the blue heron
aims through hot gray evening,
slow-swimming, to a red-pink sundisc,
as you have moved
easily, past my dry horizons,
your big flourish stirring thick air
in my spirit's summer.
You are life in stillness,
music in silence.

Sheila Cardano

Watching the Sunset

Watching the sun set on Chesapeake Bay,
Dreaming, our thoughts wander away
To familiar old places and faces we knew—
What does it matter! There's me and there's you.

We can be merry—we can be sad
Dance with the seagulls—pretend we are mad
As long as we manage to see eye to eye
And snuggle up closely, as time rushes by.

In silence we sit at the end of the day,
Watching the sun set on Chesapeake Bay.

Sheila Cardano (b. 1921, London, England) graduated from Royal Academy of Dramatic Art. She played many roles in cities of England including London. She resided in Italy for over forty years. She has been writing poetry since age 7, and has composed a book of poems for her grandchildren (unpublished). She discovered the Eastern Shore of Virginia just over two years ago and enjoys the peace of the beaches of the Chesapeake Bay.

Kathy L. Cawthon

The Battle

Last night I fought a raging poem;
A violent struggle 'twas!
It mauled me with its metaphors
And ripped me with its clause.

The lines growled, the rhythms bit,
The rhymes tore into me.
I tried to run, but was pounced upon
By a snarling simile.

It gnawed me with allusions vague
And chewed right through my soul.
My strength was gone, I fought no more,
And the poem ate me whole.

Kathy L. Cawthon (b. 1951, Teague, TX), is a freelance writer and photographer. Her "not quite light" verse has appeared in *Writer's Digest* magazine and received a number of awards. Her articles have appeared in several national publications, and her nonfiction book *The Devil's Web* was published in 1989. She is a Fellow of the Eastern Virginia Writing Project at the College of William and Mary. She lives in Hampton and is currently at work on her first novel.

Eunice de Chazeau

John Gardner O

He found the night too fine for sleep,
    all living on the rise.
He felt his two-wheeled motor leap
    and hum beneath his thighs.
How sweet the dark that reeks of spring!
    Hear the peepers singing.

Begin again at forty-nine
    new love to glint his eye,
new love to make his body shine;
    old simple love put by.
How sweet the dark that reeks of spring!
    Hear the peepers singing.

He sensed new power within him freed,
    old words he would remold.
Elation is the taste of speed
    as streaming hopes unfold.
How sweet the dark that reeks of spring!
    Hear the peepers singing.

He slurred the by-roads lap on lap
    in throbbing jubilee,
not foreseeing night would wrap
    his heart around a tree.
O still the dark that reeks of spring!
    Hear the peepers singing.

Eunice de Chazeau (b. 1905, Seattle, WA), a twenty year resident of Virginia, has published three collections of poetry and one volume of prose, her most recent, a selection of verse entitled *Born Permeable* (ROAD Publishers, 1992).

Eunice de Chazeau

Artemesia
(Before the Mausoleum in Caria)

Embraced by wind,
my back to sun and sea, I watch
where rock slopes up to fluted columns.
There throngs are dancing delight and
    strewing flowers.
Atop the colonnade
bearing its pyramid with the
    twenty-four steps,
you stand in your marble chariot
and I beside it,
light on our marble faces
slowly turning them to gold:

golden as long ago when, brother and
    sister,
we ran among the lupine, holding
    hands,
and dawdled along the sandbars of
    Meander,
our lips atingle with living;
golden as in our marriage bed
scented with roses and myrrh;
and golden as on the prow of our
    trireme
bearing down on silver seas and the
    enemy.

Mausolus, you were the sun's warmth
    on my shoulder,
and I have given your name
the saddest of all monuments.

Nets To Catch the Wind

J.P.Q. El-Fayoumy (b. 1930, New York, NY), writer and teacher, retired from Norfolk State University where she had established the Creative Writing program. In Virginia Beach, she collects poems for her work-in-progress, *Houses, Shadows*. She has written all her life, working in advertising and public relations. She keeps very much alive her roots in New York and Cape Cod, as well as in Egypt.

J.P.Q. El-Fayoumy

Winter Street
Cape Cod, 1941

Aunt Lillian's house was peanut butter
    jars, topless,
jellied glasses hardening in the angled
    sun,
coffee cups of half-consumed milk,
cranked open cans of cat food,
    remaindered, and
damp towels on a paint-splattered black
    Cape floor.
Her seven sisters, despairing,
annually traversed the Sagamore Bridge
    from their more decorous homes to
her antique three-quarter Cape on
    Winter Street, off North,
that listed on the lawn like a ship
    caught on a shallow shoal,
in order to order the playpen world of
their younger sister,
        especially the kitchen.
But the children of the sisters saw no
    wrong as they
loved and laughed and
sprawled and swarmed
into the world of this woman
whose house was
fairy tales and
Grandma's tunes
served up with doughnuts fresh from
    Main Street
and tuna fish
and bakery bread,
and after-beach shampoos of hair dried
    in the darkening sun.
Here was a secret of existence, of living,
a world where all children pulsed to
    love,
where wounds were bandaged, and
    sunburns soothed,
where cats were without fleas, and dogs
    without collars,
where rain became sun, where brass
    became gold, and where
Pennies turned to Pounds.

Eunice de Chazeau

Artemesia
(Before the Mausoleum in Caria)

Embraced by wind,
my back to sun and sea, I watch
where rock slopes up to fluted columns.
There throngs are dancing delight and
    strewing flowers.
Atop the colonnade
bearing its pyramid with the
    twenty-four steps,
you stand in your marble chariot
and I beside it,
light on our marble faces
slowly turning them to gold:

golden as long ago when, brother and
    sister,
we ran among the lupine, holding
    hands,
and dawdled along the sandbars of
    Meander,
our lips atingle with living;
golden as in our marriage bed
scented with roses and myrrh;
and golden as on the prow of our
    trireme
bearing down on silver seas and the
    enemy.

Mausolus, you were the sun's warmth
    on my shoulder,
and I have given your name
the saddest of all monuments.

J.P.Q. El-Fayoumy

Winter Street
Cape Cod, 1941

Aunt Lillian's house was peanut butter
>jars, topless,
jellied glasses hardening in the angled
>sun,
coffee cups of half-consumed milk,
cranked open cans of cat food,
>remaindered, and
damp towels on a paint-splattered black
>Cape floor.
Her seven sisters, despairing,
annually traversed the Sagamore Bridge
>from their more decorous homes to
her antique three-quarter Cape on
>Winter Street, off North,
that listed on the lawn like a ship
>caught on a shallow shoal,
in order to order the playpen world of
their younger sister,
>especially the kitchen.
But the children of the sisters saw no
>wrong as they
loved and laughed and
sprawled and swarmed
into the world of this woman
whose house was
fairy tales and
Grandma's tunes
served up with doughnuts fresh from
>Main Street
and tuna fish
and bakery bread,
and after-beach shampoos of hair dried
>in the darkening sun.
Here was a secret of existence, of living,
a world where all children pulsed to
>love,
where wounds were bandaged, and
>sunburns soothed,
where cats were without fleas, and dogs
>without collars,
where rain became sun, where brass
>became gold, and where
Pennies turned to Pounds.

J.P.Q. El-Fayoumy (b. 1930, New York, NY), writer and teacher, retired from Norfolk State University where she had established the Creative Writing program. In Virginia Beach, she collects poems for her work-in-progress, *Houses, Shadows*. She has written all her life, working in advertising and public relations. She keeps very much alive her roots in New York and Cape Cod, as well as in Egypt.

Laddie Fisher

Night is Gone

The whispering!
Whippoorwill of night has paused
To hear the movement of the leaves
Heralding dawn.
Grey streaks emerging,
Day's pyre is surging through the trees
And night is gone.

Laddie Fisher (b. 1920, Cincinnati, OH), a graduate of the University of Michigan and a retired Public Information Officer, City of Roanoke, has published two chapbooks: *My City* (1987) and *Come Walk the Mall* (1990).
Her work has appeared in numerous anthologies since 1968. She is listed in *Writers in Virginia* in poetry and fiction, and in *Who's Who in Writers, Editors & Poets*. A member of the Poetry Society of Virginia and Vice-President of the Roanoke Valley Branch of the National League of American Pen Women, she lives in Roanoke.

Linda Beth Fristoe

La Lune D'Hiver Sur Mes Seines
(Moon On My Breasts in Winter)

Only Aurora's eyes saw
dawn's new light
caress my breasts
that spring along the Seine
when I wore quiet violets
of unknown passion
beneath the whispered pink
awaiting a secret touch.

Mermaids watched wistfully
when I walked Capri in summer,
breasts born to be caressed
bared for golden kisses
from Apollo's warm mouth,
as he sought wildflowers woven
with hyacinths in scented hair
no man had ever known.

Demeter delivered rhododendron
    dreams
to cast autumn's Venetian light
across breasts aching
with the knowing of man
and the pleasure he gave
for which Persephone ever pays.
And like a molten volcano,
I waited quivering.

Until Selene sought me out
and brought me home
where he had waited
to crush an orchid
between bodies becoming one
and I allowed him to know me and
    watch
moonlight on my breasts in winter.

Linda Beth Fristoe (b. 1958, Terra Alta, WV), an honor graduate of the University of Virginia with a master's degree in English, teaches creative writing and seminars for gifted and talented students. She is an administrator in Europe for the American Council for International Studies. A resident of Front Royal, VA, she has read her poetry at Shenandoah University, Barter Theatre, and the University of Virginia. Widely published, she was named Editor's Choice by *Poet's Market*.

Linda Beth Fristoe

Midnight Monologue

Remember nights I read your rhythms,
met and matched them to mine
in our land of always summer?
You laced my hair with moonbeams
and burrowed into the furrow
of my wound
to fill me with your diamonds
and leave the garden glow
in an aura of harvest dreams.
You mounted and rode me up Orion
past deep purple mountains
cast with sunlight and silver
and made me sing in your arms
like the sea.
Love led me through the woman songs
where I wore new moonlight
and let you enter my silence
to know its willow soul.
I shall not kneel at your grave:
there is no need;
it is this empty pillow next to mine
that once saddled starlight hips
then graced your gentle head
before these nights of midnight blue.

With You

And when I die,
will you touch me again,
weave your hands through hair
that you loved gently,
hands that made our destiny dance?

Then, will you live
while I wait for you, asleep?
Allow your ears more willow songs,
your eyes their summer skies
awaiting silver rains.

Return to Rome, remember me,
and as you wander silent sands,
take pause, and with the sun reflect
upon two shadows
where you alone stand.

Linda Beth Fristoe

Endymion's Embrace

All the gypsy caravans have gone
and the final poet remains
the mateless moon awaits
Endymion's embrace.

His spirit wandered the heavens
for seven, then eleven more years
in quest of the shattered topaz eyes
he dreamed about before being born.

He moved mountains
where lions lived among pearls
and strode silent seas
as mermaids watched
wearing tears
for the moon maid.

Across relentless midnights he came
to mount the maid riding rainbows
until skies were transformed
to shooting stars.

Within his emerald embrace
she told him the candles,
like the caravans, had gone.
He whispered, "We'll make love
by the light from your eyes.
Now, cast aside your angel wings
and wear wild animal wants
in our nether bed tonight."
And in that night she trusted,
opening like a flower to ask,
"Do you see the colors
of sunlight and starbursts,
or a quiet cave quivering in darkness?"
Leading her into the deep, silver climax,
he breathed, "I see you."

Wondrous twilights waned
as she wove tales of longer moons
until one misty morn,
he caressed her goodbye breasts
and like a memory moved on.
Now, her song is so silent
that even the roses ache.

Gertrude Gunther

Partridgeberry
mitchella repens

Twin flowers combine
ovary with ovary
bearing a single berry
on May woodland vine

so our mutuality
births a drupe of pleasure
as from my taboret
you take up a book unknown to you
and read silently;
silent too,
I hope you'll like the author;
you (sensible of my feeling?) begin
reading aloud and read to chapter's end.

Common Mullein, Icon
verbascum thapsus

green rectitude of ramrod stalk
and ascension of terminal spire

perfection
of cinquefoiled flowers

holy index finger pointing up,
of stem leaf

Gertrude Gunther (b. 1911, Mexico City, Mexico) studied poetry at Barnard College. Living on Virginia's Eastern Shore in Onancock the past twenty-three years, she celebrates the region with poetry booklets, among them *Pussyfooting through Nature*. Her poems have appeared in *The Christian Science Monitor*, the *Anthology of Poems by Member Poets*, Poetry Society of Virginia (1985), and *The Poet's Domain*, Vols. 1, 2, 3, 4, and 5.

Gertrude Gunther

"The Coffee's Cold." "It Always Is."

Two nursing home ancients
away from bedside anchorage
lunch in the hallway
at a small table connecting
one figure to the other:
white hair, white skin,
white gowns: white marble
sculpture in the round; the
stone reflecting light
at surfaces of deeper lying
crystals.

Anne Hawes

The Small Person

We met with love, immediate, complete,
When Tonykin was three;
He gave me a spool of thread,
His eyes were free
Of guile, devoid of dread,
My instant friend of three.

We met with love and old familiar hugs.
When Tony Wells was four;
He drew "4" backwards in the sand,
Then dragged me off, imperative of
    hand
To see his turtle—
That day when he was four.

We met with love, shouting in the wind
When Anthony was five;
I gave him cookies fresh from off the
    stove;
We flew our kites and laughed,
So glad to be alive,
I and my friend of five!

We met with love, a bit reserved and shy
When Anthony Wells was nine;
He managed to say, "Hi!"
And grin;
this gap-toothed friend of mine
Stood up and shook my hand—
When he was nine.

Anne Hawes (b. 1918, Mt. Vernon, NY) lives in a retirement community in Alexandria, VA, after a career in social work and teaching. She has been writing for twenty-five years, but this is her debut in print. She is currently working on a book of poems to be called *Wing the Blue Deep*.

Barbara McKay Hewin

Gray

I feel alone today,
my friendly ghosts all wander other
    worlds,
the streets are foggy and the trees are
    gray,
and raw depression round my spirit
    curls
like hungry snakes about a dying bird.

Beauty is what I crave—
the perfect rose by perfect thought
    designed,
the flow of velvet, starlight on the
    waves,
a baby's kiss, and dancing—lots of
    dance,
to joy-filled music of romantic minds.

I need to stretch my soul,
to feel a sentient God behind my eyes,
to justify the dancing and preserve the
    rose,
to understand some smitch of human
    goals,
and send new verses through uncharted
    skies.

April Rain

The iridescent days of youth slip by
and fall like drops of April rain
that shimmer crystal down the pane
where there is nothing to detain
them as they dry.

And yet it seems their liquid symmetry
leaves patterns on the dusty pane,
memorials of silver stain
that moonlight filters through again
in filigree.

Barbara McKay Hewin (b. 1927, New York, NY)—poet, costumer for many stage productions, and homemaker—won a 1st Place award in the Virginia A.A.U.W. poetry contest. Her poems have appeared in *The Poet's Domain*, Vols. 1, 2, 3, 4, 5, and in *Poetic Voices of America*, Sparrowgrams Poetry Forum, Inc. She is listed in the Directory of Virginia Writers and continues writing from her home in Williamsburg, VA.

Alana Maubury Hunter

Trained to Shoot Off

Pause from the guns,
The drill of existence.
Remove your eye from the scope
And hear
Deafening mindless mutterings
Of appropriate words shot off,
Leaden with the hollow stock
Of sentimental justification.
Remove finger from the trigger
And listen
To unbroken rapidfire
Of tactful, fashionable utterance.
See billows of smoke
Of bromides bursting in air,
Unchallenged by a glottal breath of
    truth.

The battle bellows behind you
As you walk away.
Your wound of wellness
Burns
In the face of perpetual ills.

Glimpse

A black room
My eyes closed
An illusionary arch of you
Is over me
And gone with the same breath,
But lingers hard—
And closed eyes
Ram back
A glimpse.

Alana Maubury Hunter (b. 1962, Allentown, PA), winner of the F. Lyman Windolf Award in 1980, is an artist, calligrapher, and human rights lobbyist. She recently returned from a fact-finding mission, lead by former presidential candidate, John Anderson, to Syria, Jordan, Israel and the occupied territories. Her home and studio are currently located in Arlington, VA.

Agnes Nasmith Johnston

Valley of Grief

Tear drops rim my eyes
when sorrow engulfs me
as I press my fingers
against throbbing temples.

A maple branch scratches my window
and I focus beyond darkness
to russet hills above the valley.

A woodpecker drums
in the wild cherry tree,
his beat vibrating
through my pain—

    I turn to bake
    my daily bread.

Brush Strokes

Easels side by side
we brushed meadow springs,
mountain or river
across our paintings.

Our views flowed
in harmonious hues,
blending values,
opposites and complements.

Now you've moved
to another realm,
mixing oil and turpentine,
stroking harsh design.

I lean over my watercolor,
tears spotting river and ridge
    while I wonder—
    was granite always hiding
in the darkness of our bridge?

Agnes Nasmith Johnston (b. 1921, Huchow, China) has had poems in every volume of *The Poet's Domain*. Her first book of poetry, *Beyond the Moongate* (Lotus Press) came out in 1987 with another printing in 1989. She continues to write poems about her return to China in 1988 and has recently been published in *Black Buzzard Review*, *The China Connection*, *The Hollins Critic*, *The Lyric*, and *Midwest Poetry Review*. She is listed in *Writers in Virginia*.

Agnes Nasmith Johnston

Refugees

Abraham's children
struggle up jagged ranges
above the valleys of war,
shielding their children
from rock, mud, and snow.

Their tears drop
on sick babies,
the weak, and aged.

Who will bring sustenance
to the innocents
in alien mountains,
and the plains of Mesopotamia?

Carrie Jackson Karegeannes

Dupont Circle

Zorba Cafe,
Tiny, crowded tables,
Taped zoubouki music,
Steaming cinnamon-scented moussaka,
Black olives, feta cheese,
Fragments of Greek phrases long
    not heard—
But blue and gold and white of Greece
Are only memories now.

And yet—and yet—
Once more I hear your laughter.

More Than Music

Yes, "music heard with you was more
    than music,"
Bread more than bread.
Even when you turned from me,
Your presence gave objects in that room,
Trees along those streets,
Their life, their reason for being.
The day's light, the new spring's joy,
The vividness, the reality,
Their very imprint on the world,
Were because you knew them.

And now music's meaning
Is in the memory of you,
And bread is tasteless—
Unless by chance a croissant on a
    tiny balcony
Above a sycamore-shaded square
    a summer day in Arles,
Or at a shaky sidewalk table
Pressed by Paris throngs,
Brings
    fleetingly
        your voice.

Carrie Jackson Karegeannes (b. 1923, Wusih, China) first appeared in *The Poet's Domain*, in Vol. 4, *A Bundle of Grief...a Shovel of Stars*, and followed in Vol. 5, *A Sense of Ocean and Old Trees*. A retired editor-writer for newspapers and government agencies, she has written verse all her life, her earliest publication coming in 1942 in *Young Texas Sings*. She has lived in Paris and Athens, as well as China, and now makes her home in Annandale, VA.

Jean P. Klotzbach

By the Opera House

There's a certain corner in Chicago
Where the local men love to wait,
To see all kinds of ladies
Meet a very special fate.

As the wind roars in like a demon
Female garments fly away.
The men lay bets on their little pets
As to what rides where today.

The matrons old and not so bold
Frantically grab for skirts and dresses,
But the sweet young things grab for
 their hats
So as not to disturb their tresses!

The Wind

What may catch the wind?
A windmill's lazy arms or a soaring
 bird,
A drifting feather, a speeding plane,
An echo not yet heard.

What joy she brings to life
Lifting golden pollen to a flower's
 waiting face,
Carrying God-given rain
To every desperate, arid place.

Terror she may also bring—
Death, destruction, and despair.
Take not the wind too lightly, friend
She has many moods. Beware!

Jean P. Klotzbach (b. 1921, Buffalo, NY) has travelled extensively with career and family and presently resides in Columbia, MD. She enjoys writing poetry and short stories and looks forward to each day's new experiences in living.

Olive S. Lanham

March Moon

The magic gold-white glory
    of the full spring moon
pours down on blackened trees
    and shadowed lawns.

I stand quite motionless and feel
    cool touch of moonlight on my skin,
and breathe the damp fresh spicy
    fragrance
    of the garden after dark.

Winter Menu

A bowl of stars for breakfast
    with a plate of cloud ice cream.
A rainbow parfait sunrise,
    and a cold drink from a stream.

Icicles on bush and tree—
    sweet crystal popsicles for me,
as down long mountain roads we go
    making whipped cream angels in
    the snow!

Olive S. Lanham (b. 1924, Soochow, China) attended Shanghai American School and Duke University. She has lived thirty-five years in Silver Spring, MD. A writer of short stories and a play, she sold her first poem at age six. She has been published by Southern Poetry Association, (Pass Christian, MS) and by the Florida State Poetry Association. Now working on a book of family letters, she enjoys Daytona Beach, traveling, and Chinese origami.

Mary Antil Lederman

Parlor Talk
(Arachnida Non Grata)

With such painstaking artistry you
 weave each slender strand—
More delicate than finest lace your
 dainty fairyland.

You ply your silken warp and woof of
 fragile *macramé*
As deftly as a Claude Monet in
 sheltered *atelier*...

Movements measured, slow, precise,
 unhurried, as if sure,
Once completed, your masterpiece will,
 like great art, endure.

I hold your small fate in my hands—a
 power not guilt-free
While cognizant another Hand wields
 my frail destiny.

Though in control of your demise—and
 helpless with my own—
Please, know it's nothing personal, this
 sad *sine qua non*.

Why did you pick *my* windowsill for
 your inspired loom
And force me with my vacuum scythe,
 alas, to reap your doom?

Mary Antil Lederman (b. 1925, Los Angeles, CA), a retired foreign-language teacher and former department head in Charlottesville, VA, graduated from Syracuse University and earned a master's degree at the University of Virginia. In addition to national prizes, she has won six PSVA poetry prizes since becoming a member of the Poetry Society of Virginia in 1989. Her work has appeared in *Albemarle* magazine, *The Charlottesville Observer*, VRTA *Broadcast, Poetic Voices of America, Treasured Poems of America*, 1991, 1992, *Orphic Lute* and Vols. 2, 3, 4, and 5, of *The Poet's Domain*.

Mary Antil Lederman

China in Mourning
(Winter, 1989)

  White, docile pandas
in Beijing Zoo catch snowflakes
  on hot, eager tongues...

  Spring's ardor snuffed out
with the brave, white-shirted youth
  who defied the tanks.

  Tiananmen Square
lies chill beneath ermine shroud
  in the winter cold...

  White-draped catafalque
on which Freedom reposes
  frozen...moribund...

  Its blood-spattered stones
clad in funereal white—
  like China's young hopes.

Holding Tight...
With Open Arms...
(Sonnet to my Sons)

If I could keep spring eternal, would I?
A rose would hold its budding glory
  fair,
And heady perfumed freshness ever
  wear—
Never to wither brown away and die.
If I could preserve innocence, would I?
A tiny infant safely tethered there,
Dependent always on maternal care—
My presence ever needed and nearby?

Without dry petals there'd be no sachet,
Evoking thoughts of vibrant beauty
  past—
Captured essence enhanced in this
  fragrance.
Without maturing, minds would arid
  stay—
Creating no *chefs-d'oeuvre* to outlast
Mortal time in more perfect permanence.

John Long

Tree-Dreaming

A bed made with boards
and a twig beneath your pillow
will nestle you in the hollow
of a tree's December dream.
Faint it will seem at first
until you learn to go deeper,
flowing down like sap in autumn
under the forest floor
to where your spirit winters.
You, in your woody reverie,
will not pine for vision
but will learn to see in weathers,
and to feel in the slow emotions
that people call the seasons.
Sublimely trusting dayshine
to enlighten our clairvoyant hair,
you'd not think it ridiculous
to drink with your toes.
Sporadical compulsions
you used to know as winds
will pass like invisible queens,
making your skeleton bow.
If you dream of spring's return,
you'll feel your blood start to climb,
and your hands may begin to open
in a new but familiar way.
And if you should sense something
like a close crackle of static,
like electric smoke or an echoing spark
that lingers just in your shadow,
don't be alarmed, but realize
your tree is dreaming of you.

John Long (b. 1947, Richmond, VA) taught English at Virginia Polytechnic Institute and now works as an editor for the General Assembly in Richmond.

John Long

The Glad Insomniac

Long-awaited darkness
dawns at twilight,
grows clearer with haze,
dethrones the upstart colors,
and rescues the day from warmth.

Night does not fall, but rises,
unfurling in space like a perfect flag
featuring stars and a moon
and shadowing whole hemispheres
into new alliances.

Evening's a blessed curtain
drawn across the window world,
eclipsing the day's excesses,
shielding the eyes from glitter,
and shedding on error's glare
a little lack of light.

Yes, and the moon makes tides
in the mind's sluggish sea,
flooding the hidden harbors,
washing the secret shores,
where thought and memory wait
for a current to send them sailing.

John Long

Geographic

To elevate my point of view,
I each night in dreams ascend
a mountain of the moon,
from which observatory
I'm able to discern
what fills the space between us.

Believe me when I tell you
it is only a curve of earth
—only forests, rivers, towns,
    some meadows and a bay
—only a little distance
    of old, known terrain.
Comes daylight we descend to earth,
my dreams and I, like paratroops
in chutes of turned-over tears.
Down and down through the dawn we
    come—
it's hard to keep a few regrets
from catching in the treetops—
but most of our landings are tender.

This rising up, this falling back
is hardly news to you.
But can you feel me at daybreak
staring through your horizon?
I seek a path, a passage,
lost and long grown over,
that once I knew by heart.

Michael Hugh Lythgoe

Nets

It does not seem so long ago
When we bathed our first born
In a blue ocean and the sun
Of a summer near Lisboa, Portugal.

The cold Atlantic waves made
Our baby boy cry out. It was
His first shock from chilling brine
He would soon learn to swim in
    unafraid.

The fishermen of Nazare
Rowed their daily earnings
Back to the beach in brightly painted
    boats.
They wore long, black stocking caps the
    way

Deep pockets keep possessions dry and
    safe.
With baggy, plaid pants rolled
To their knees, they waded in the surf,
To bring waiting wives, who wore
    black, sun-drying fish

For the whitewashed village, and then
    mended their nets.
Our son does not remember those
    fishermen
In that world of black and white. He
    was very young;
But as he grew, he saw Caribbean
    seamen's nets

And shrimp boats in sunsets off the
    Florida keys,
Sampled *tapas* in Seville during Holy
    Week,
And trekked the Cornish coast; he has
Flown over oceans between the North
    Sea

And the Chesapeake where crabbers
    use no nets.

Michael Hugh Lythgoe (b. 1941, Evansville, IN), who lives in Gainesville, VA, recently read some of his poems at the newly opened Painter Gallery on Virginia's Eastern Shore. He has served with the Air Force in Vietnam, Europe, Latin America and the Caribbean. Mike's poems have appeared in Vols. 4 and 5 of *The Poet's Domain* and recently in *The Eclectic Literary Forum*, *Lullwater Review* (Emory), *View From The Edge* (The National Library of Poetry, MD, 1992), and *The Reston Review*. In 1992 critic and author, Edward Butscher, selected one of his poems, in national competition, to be part of an exhibit of poetry and visual art on the theme of heroism at the Peconic Gallery in Long Island, NY.

Michael Hugh Lythgoe

Now this son who first cringed from the
    sea in Portugal
Sets sail in his untried craft, with his
    bride:
Sailor preparing to harvest life's catch
    with his nets.

for Michael and Amy

Ballad for Forsythia

The sun daubs yellow, makes April's
    flower.
The wind is lion-like at the tail of a kite.
Flashy floods spill the frogs and worms
    ashore.
The silver drizzle is licking awake the
    light.
The street, sleek as a seal, swims black
    and bright,
As the thickets explode and our senses
    cloud;
The stunning new growth is shocking to
    our sight:
The forsythia shrub is lemon loud.

We breath in the swampy scents of
    muddy season;
The ripening aromas we know
Are whiffs of a resurrection passing
    reason,
Wilting in instants, as blooms go;
Our focus flashes. We miss the golden
And greening shoots uncoil, the bold
    show
Of mustard erupting in commotion—
The forsythia shrub is lemon loud.

So soon do hearts deafen, we hardly feel
The thrilling brush of feather, buff of
    cloud.
Before we turn too blind to birth, be still!
The forsythia shrub is lemony and loud.

Michael Hugh Lythgoe

Long Key

Orion travels over sea-rattles
Of the January night.
The Hunter is a myth over Miami—
Slain for a love he craves in starry space.
He patrols planets above a spray-wet
    jetty
Where we lie like driftwood
Burls entwined on rocky coast
Beside the flashing buoy
Blinking survival codes
To astronomers navigating in the keys.
Banished Orion's shadow crosses
    Havana's
Searching floodlights spotting
    afterburners'
Flames, as gunboats prowl
    revolutionary reefs.
The Hunter faces fierce snorts
In "the bull ring of the moon,"
Poised to pierce in over the horns
To the stellar heart of Taurus.

Orion, exiled to the galaxies,
Doomed by Diana's jealousy, lights up
The Florida Straits, shines
Above the fighter pilot's sparks
Scarring the lunar face with their flights.
Stirring the sweet, black *cafecito*-night.

There are scraping sounds
Of keels aground on coral,
Spanish sobs washing
In from beyond the breakers.
Cubans are slapping down
Their dominoes—white dots in ebony
On *Calle Ocho*. Orion roams above
Our archipelago seeking the cutlass-cut
Cane squeezed into rum, to taste;
He sips the sea-breeze of the keys,
The uncertain freedoms
Of a wretched refugee.

Barbara Mabe

A Boy's God

Once I heard a boy explain God to
    someone else.
"Me and god are 'just like that!'" he said,
    holding up two fingers.
"Me and God are brothers.
I talk to God. God talks to me.
We talk about each other.

"Sometimes we hum a little tune.
Sometimes we sing out loud.
Sometimes we only think together.
    No words.
We listen to each other think.

"Me and God, we stick together.
We walk side by side.
Nobody can get us then.
We stick up for one another.
Me and God are close, you know.
Me and God are brothers."

Barbara Mabe (b. 1931, Wichita, KS), painter and art educator, takes inspiration from deep meditation on nature. She has created three books of meditative writings: *The Plight of Children, Tiger Woman Wildly Running,* and *Male and Female*. She is a member of the National League of American Pen Women. Her paintings hang in private and corporate collections throughout Virginia. Formerly of Richmond, she now resides in Wake, VA.

Joan Maloof

Breathing with Daddy

So daddy, this is for you.
A few words which will never know
the vibration of air.
Some ancient history about how,
lying in your bed in the morning,
the air became you.

How, in an effort to be like you,
I drew my breath in unison,
willing my fragile rib cage to expand,
refusing my heart's cry for release.

How could a human hold air so sacred?
You, daddy, in your dreams,
the deep breaths only etching
some escape or evasion, you
were unaware of the wide awake child,
who innocently believed in the sanctity
of an exhalation.

But I never could hold the air long
 enough.
It was just one more thing beyond my
 control.
And I failed you even in your sleep.

Joan Maloof (b. 1956, Wilmington, DE) is a naturalist living in a riverside farmhouse near the small town of Quantico, on Maryland's Eastern Shore. She has a special interest in plants, both wild and cultivated. This poem is part of a manuscript entitled *Our Gold is Not Ordinary Gold*.

Dorothy W. Millner

Island Therapy

I burrow into sand
seeking shells
murmurs of other seas
Damp air licking
envelopes long sealed
chambers of my mind

Yellowed sheets spread
open to sun and sand
old shadows fray,
drift as grey gulls
wind-lifted
leaving no marker

Time's Fool

Architect fashioned
flesh and blood
for birth and death
forever ending
forever replenished

City of the mind
electric impulses
crossed wires
sudden sparks
sputtering into silence.

Loss of feeling:
the stillness of
an inert idea
in an unread book.

Dorothy W. Millner (b. , Pittsburgh, PA) graduated from Sarah Lawrence college, earned a Ph.D. degree from The Graduate Center: City University of New York, and taught literature at Pace University, Pleasantville, NY. She moved to Alexandria, VA, in 1975 to work for the Federal government on various management analysis and writing projects. Now retired, she teaches literature at the Learning and Retirement Institute, George Mason University, and makes her poetry debut in this edition.

Medea E. Minnich

Encounter at the Agri-Service

I was affronted by her presence
didn't know why a woman
would want to drive a fertilizer truck
in spring

She greeted me like a bosom buddy
then said
"Friday is the big ONE"

Friday the big one, what could it mean?
I looked down at my work
pretending not to be
not in the know

"Do you know what that means?"
I didn't.

"Friday is my birthday"

Oh, I laughed nervously
then guessed out loud her Friday age to
    be
thirty
just like mine

Suddenly we were
sisters, friends, compeers
in a male place
and I
shocked at my fear
of intimacy with
one
so freshly real.

Medea E. Minnich (b. 1962, Oakland, MD), studied English and philosophy at Hood College in Frederick, MD. She enjoys painting and is presently working on a children's story. This edition marks her poetry debut.

Robert R. Montgomery

Incarnation

I saw you, father, only yesterday,
as I was passing by a store
its window showing pictures of the way
the passersby appeared; and more,
it sketched the character of every one,
uncovered things we'd hid before,
and bared in piercing flash of noonday
    sun
the fabric of our inner core.

How could you be the one reflecting
    there?
I saw you lying lifeless, neared
to offer up an unaccustomed prayer,
then paused a moment briefly cheered
to know your pain was gone, your
    struggle done.
Yet there you stood, you'd reappeared.
How natural you looked, how like your
    son;
you wore my clothes, my shoes, my
    beard.

I see you often now and know the
    thread
of DNA you passed to me
was only lent, you hold it still. This head
I thought was mine alone and free
to create thoughts, develop attitudes
was yours at first, and now I see
you guide behind the scenes, your self
    intrudes
in glimpses, momentarily.

I wonder if I ever haunt my sons
and show myself in fleeting glance
on mirrored surfaces, those special ones
that flash within. Is there a chance
that even now, before I die, they'll see
a brief awareness of the stance
of father there? Will they see you with
    me
in insight's evanescent trance?

Robert R. Montgomery (b. 1923, Quantico, VA), practiced cardiology in Bethesda, MD, until he retired to live with his wife aboard their 30-foot sailboat. In 1988, they moved ashore to their present home in Hartfield, VA. He has written many articles for medical and boating journals, but now concentrates on writing poetry. His poems have appeared in *The Southside Sentinel* and *Pleasant Living* magazine; and one was awarded first prize at the Chesapeake Writers' Conference in 1991.

Geneva Ingram Nasworthy

Chalice Holder

Alexander led
carousing discourses (symposia)
holding a calix,
(round bottomed cup), unable
to set it down,
filled.

I move about
in this symposium, and hold
—as we all do—
the calix that cannot be put
down until it's
empty.

I watch with
interest, terror and pity
to see others
drink, or dash their cups
to the stained
ground.

Tiger

Attempting to time-capsule
our tabby
as he sleeps
in his backyard green pasture,
I begin to wonder:

Photos soon bleach,
but surely a few good words
could sketch
and frame Tiger
in his fourteenth year.

October sunlight
could serve
as Oligocene amber,
trapping him
like an embedded insect.

Perhaps I am tempted to a task

Geneva Ingram Nasworthy (b. 1921, Minburn, IA) graduated from Cornell College of Iowa, was an airline stewardess, is a mother of five. Having called Chicago, Alaska Territory, Long Island, and Lebanon home, and retired from Licensed Practical Nursing, she now resides in Woodstock, VA. During her long career of writing, her poems have appeared in numerous publications.

Geneva Ingram Nasworthy

overweaning and impossible.

Even now the geologic gum
flakes and erodes,
the sun cools,
and my ink fades.

Julie Vakos Nordstrom

Birth

Slowly the infant emerges
as contracting mother's hands
grip the wooded side rails.
From the dark safe cavity
comes the reluctant tiny person
clinging to its known world.

Gently hands guide the passage
from dark into light
shocking her gasping breath.
Like newness dawning
she opens her eyes.

City Scene

Litter bag sits beside small huddled
woman in black coat and tattered
sneakers, head bent down. Tuned out.

Long legs sprint around the corner
of the skyscraper, catch the
green light, headset on. Tuned out.

Simultaneous sirens fill the air as
firetrucks run the red light, connect
to hydrant near the huddled human.
    Tuned out.

A false alarm. The jogger is gone.
With a glance at the bag lady
I walk on.

Julie Vakos Nordstrom (b. 1936, Lake Toxaway, NC), a former teacher, librarian, business manager, and bookseller makes her poetry debut with this edition. She writes at her home in Jamesville, VA, on the Eastern Shore where she has lived for 30 years.
A graduate of the College of William and Mary, she published a pictorial history, *The Eastern Shore of Virginia in Days Past* (1981). She is currently compiling a similar book to include poems and legends. She enjoys photography and travel.

Daisy Oblinger

Lord of the Harvest

If a farmer ever prays,
it is in haytime,
weather being what it is
and hay.
It takes a mighty hand
to hold back the clouds
when storms gather
in the nineties heat,
to hold the winds to west
until the ready hay
is cut
cured,
windrowed
bailed
hauled
and stored
in the hayshed
filling it with smells of summer.
Only then, let the petition rest
and rain pounce
on the steaming roof.

Daisy Oblinger (b. 1916, Amherst Co., VA) is a member of the Poetry Society of Virginia.

David J. Partie

Looking for Pebbles on Moonstone Beach

For thirty years I watched him bend,
legs washed in waves,
sifting though pebbles on Moonstone Beach,
like a jeweler, filling his coffee cans
with mottled, marbled stones
that were lit by the glint of the sinking sun,
slinging the flawed and lightless ones toward sea.
He would try to lead his son along the beach
into the shallows where the surf
would fizz and foam around his feet;
"The spot to find the finest stones," he said.
Instead I would make pock marks in the sea-drunk sand
toward the shriveled jellyfish,
the tangled ropes of purple seaweed
that would pop between my fingers,
the bone-white driftwood sandpapered smooth by time.
I did not have his patience nor his expert eye
to scrutinize the veins and contours of every stone
spilled from the Pacific.
Instead I would follow the glide and swoop of gulls,
fascinated by the shadow
of their wings against the sun,
listening to their shrieks
that filled the space between us.
For thirty years he also gathered well
the stones for the mosaic of his life.
Not all were gems, but I would often envy
the home he built with equal parts
of love and lumber, his bedrock character,
and the canning jars on his mantlepiece,
full of pebbles that once rolled

David J. Partie (b. 1944, Detroit, MI) won the Poetry Society of Virginia's Karma Deane Ogden Prize in 1991 for his poem "For the Suicide of Hart Crane" and was a first prize winner in the 1991 Lynchburg Poetry Festival for "The Landscape of Memory." He received his Ph.D. in Comparative Literature from the University of Southern California. He lives in Lynchburg, VA. and teaches German and English at Liberty University, where he also serves as Chairman of the Department of Modern Languages.

David J. Partie

across continents of waves into his
    hands.

The Whiteness of the Page

In my study
I sit and stare
at a piece
of white paper—
unlined,
unmarked,
without margins,
without face.
White as milk,
white as
trackless snow,
white as Ahab's whale—
and just as evil.
Inscrutable,
ineffable,
untamable,
untamed.
I attack it fiercely,
harpooning it with words
flung from typewriter keys.
But it resists my efforts
to imprint it with my image
and remains
as white and elusive
as sea foam
and just as silent.

Jennifer Peachey

The Autistic Child

The frail child sits in a field
of maples, blond hair streaming behind
her in the breeze.
Year after year she rocks back and forth,
humming in time with her
movement;
a calculated concert
only she has the music to.

The trees isolate her
from the images beyond their branches.
Knowing not what exists outside this
    circle of green—
she has never felt the
white snow melt on her warm skin,
never waded in the teal tides of an
incoming ocean.

The seedlings come closer to nestle
her deeper in the narrowing field.
Twigs stroke her long,
blond braids all the while.

And when the snow falls,
not one flake melts upon her icy skin.

Jennifer Peachey (b. 1974, Shelby, NC), a freshman at Virginia Intermont College, plans to major in art and creative writing. She enjoys painting and ballet and currently resides in Bristol. She gave her first poetry reading at Shenandoah University during her senior year of high school. She has been published in *Virginia Writing* and in *ApaEros* and *Athena Incognito* magazines.

Richard Raymond, III

Cradle Song

When all my toys are put away,
My nursery darkened for the night,
I'll sleep, remembering the day,
And dream of golden morning light,

Seeming to drift through halls of cloud,
Approach a vast and shining throne.
A great voice speaks my name aloud,
Inquires of all that I have done,

A father-voice, majestic, clear,
Bidding me tell of my misdeeds—
I stand in childlike awe and fear,
Wishing to sink beneath the weeds.

In one pathetic, saving thought
I whisper, "Surely I have sinned,
But see—these wings of verse I wrought,
They soared, they danced upon the
  wind."

Richard Raymond, III (b. 1930, Cambridge, NY) a graduate of U.S. Naval Academy, served in the U.S. Marine Corps. His poems have appeared in *Army Times*, *Leatherneck*, *Infantry*, and *Naval Institute Proceedings*, and three previous issues of *The Poet's Domain*. An engineering technician, he has won three 1st place awards in 1992 World Order of Narrative & Formalist Poets and has had four poems in the 1961 Civil War anthology *From Sumter to Appomattox*.

Evelyn Ritchie (b. 1927, Criders, VA) was the first member of her family to attend high school and then graduated from Bridgewater College at the age of 19. She served as a Presbyterian missionary from 1952-1966, and has been a teacher in Richmond Public Schools for the years following. She is the author of a poetry volume, *Hickory Sled*, and of numerous poems, articles, and stories in magazines. At present she lives in Richmond and participates in literary activities.

Evelyn Ritchie

Hero of Richmond Theater Fire, 1811

Slave Gilbert Hunt, passing to his
    shop-loft
After night church, hears the unearthly
    screams
Of people trapped inside, looks for a soft
Mattress to land on if they jumped;
    Hell's gleams
Provide no help. The only window's
    high.
He holds his arms out, catches as they
    fly,

Twelve fortunates. Flames lick around
    McCaw
The last, flung senseless into strong
Skilled blacksmith's grip. Only next
    day, in awe,
Can he guess how the man bore him
    along
Alive, all the way home through icy
    streets.
Many have died, but one brave note
    repeats—

Hunt is a hero. Now the *Richmond Whig*
Praises his ingenuity and strength,
Expresses hope that his reward be big:
Freedom, no less. A fund's begun. At
    length,
His story's published but its scant
    proceeds
Fall short of the eight hundred Gilbert
    needs.

He works the iron harder than before;
"My days are numbered, Lord—let
    some be free!"
Whatever's hammered in the whitehot
    roar
Of Gilbert's forge beats like a heavy sea
On rocky slavery. In doubletime,
He raps and tempers rungs that he must
    climb,

Evelyn Ritchie

And reaches liberty. "When others fall
Short of your goal," he thinks, "then
    you must buy
Yourself to own yourself. A
    blacksmith's maul
Strikes freedom if you never let it lie."

"I Myself and no Other"

*"God himself, whom I shall see with
my eyes, I myself and no other"*—Job 19:26-27

Every *I* beholds You,
Hand tightening the vise:
I the priest, who offers
For these merry scoffers
My children, sacrifice;
I, the just and rational
Model fair-employer,
Calling You, Destroyer,
The last unanswerable
Master of beasts and men;
I the loath survivor
Daring You, Conniver,
To blot me from Your ken;
I, unthankful friend
Suffering new renditions
Of trite suppositions,
Letting my trial end
Unjudged and imprecise;
I the squelched defendant
Clasping Your transcendent
Hand loosening the vise.

Evelyn Ritchie

The Giver

For Mother Teresa of Calcutta and of the world

Like a prayer wheel
Her blood spins
Its systolic
Disciplines;
Love of Jesus
Jessamines
Filthy dying
Scabrous skins.

A vigil given,
A prayer apiece,
She guides the last
And least toward peace.
Who like this saint,
Midwife Therese,
Can deliver
Heaven's increase
Without flagging,
Without cease?

Ada G. Sanderson

Thoreau's Walk In Winter

adapted from
Henry D. Thoreau's "A Winter Walk"

In the powdery snow
Of a Concord winter
Thoreau sets out.

He finds the Bell-like frosty air
Pure and stinging,
An elixir to the lungs.

He muses how nature
Nurtures plants and animals
To withstand the cold.

He notes God-like strength
In the tops of mountains
Holding forth their pristine pureness.

From the altar of the breast
A subterranean fire warms him
Kindled by the embers of a winter sun.

He finds a canopy of pines
Covered and closed in snow
Cheery with eternal summer.

Mice and rabbits
Grown strong from arctic nights
Stir with life towards light.

He sees the pickerel fisherman
Blending with the woods and hills
Belonging to the natural family of man.

Clouds gather and snow falls
    incessantly.
Curls of smoke from a distant hearth
Beckon him home.

He observes how effortlessly
Snow covers his footprints
And blocks out all traces of man.

Ada G. Sanderson (b. 1921, Washington, DC), poetry teacher, Fairfax County Adult and Community Education, lives in Falls Church, VA, with her six cats who alternately act as muses and distractions to her efforts as a poet. She is a member of the Poetry Society of Virginia and won their Karma Deane Ogden Memorial first prize in 1990.

Askold Skalsky

Loves's Platform

Let's make believe that we are happy.
Let's build a foundation of bliss
On which the empire of our daily life
Can crumble into consciousness.
When we refute the authority
Of our mere minds
And the oppression
Of our eyes,
What can be obliterated
Except memory?
What should be forgotten
Except familiarity?
Freedom now!

Taking Stock

This is my house

And in it stand
my table, chairs,
my cabinet of food.

Here are my suits and shirts,
my shelves of books.

This is my yard and trees,
my cat asleep
upon the steps.

This is my son.

And these
are my gray hairs
which,

when I die,

will go on growing
for a little while
before they

stop.

Askold Skalsky (b. 1940, Ukraine),
lives in Ijamsville, MD,
and teaches at
Hagerstown Junior College.

Barbara Smith

Hebrew Class

Penina, teacher of Hebrew
To Black Ethiopian Jews
Settling in Israel—
At absorption center
On Galilee's shore

Penina, dark hair and eyes
Warm, relays language
Through questions,
Traditions and songs

Bright-eager young men
Respond to questions—
Women reticent—
During Shabbat lighting ceremony
A young mother falters on words of
 prayer—
The class coaches—she smiles, continues

Penina says she uses electricity on
 Shabbat
Class disagrees, breaks out in native
 Amharic
To discuss issue avidly among
 themselves
They want their pictures taken after
 class
Pose, put arms around one another
Smiling, eager to please, happy
Affectionate, thankful

Barbara Smith (b. 1936, Newport News, VA) writes poetry, non-fiction, and fiction. She has published in *Orphic Lute, Currents, Great American Poetry Anthology, Cube Literary Magazine, Flights of Fancy,* and *Fictitious and True.* She won a poetry award at Christopher Newport College Writers' Conference. A member of Virginia Writers' Club, VCCA Writers in Virginia, Poetry Society of Virginia and Tidewater Writers' Association, she is a docent at the Mariner's Museum and works on a crisis telephone hotline. She visited and shot video in Tibet, Inner Mongolia, and other parts of China in 1991. She resides in Newport News, VA.

Bruce Souders (b. 1920, Richland, PA) a retired United Methodist Minister and a past president of the Poetry Society of Virginia, lives in Winchester, VA, where he is Professor Emeritus in Humanities at Shenandoah University. His poetry has appeared in *The Poet's Domain*, Vols. 3, 4, and 5. His pageant—*A Campmeeting Fly Remembers Mt. Gretna*—opened the Centennial of the Mt. Gretna Campmeeting Association in Pennsylvania, and he has edited a collection of the poems of S. Gordden Link, scheduled for publication this fall.

Bruce Souders

Plea for an Oracle

Masada: ruin in the desert! Are you
symbol of a moment of glory or silent
setting for an absurd drama, plotless
and meaningless, but worthy of
    excavation?
We browse for history in your remains;
but if we learn from suffering, what
does your suffering say to us?

What suffering should we study in
    careful detail?
The two-pronged fear of Herod: that
    Jews
would replace him with former kings,
that Antony would grant Cleopatra's
    wish
to possess Judea? The fear of besieged
defenders who died in their mutual
    resolve
never to lose their liberty?

What loss should we mourn through
    artifacts?
The glory of Herod, sumptuous,
    indulgent,
secure? The messianic hopes
of Zealots defiant of obstacles,
confirmed to sacrificial living?
The Dead Sea, silent as Baal
in the valley below offers no answers.

Under Spring Skies

Beginning a lazy
slow climb
at tether's end,
one lone kite
lightly clothed
in multicolors
competes with clouds
it cannot reach.

Bruce Souders

Early Summer: An Alpine Epiphany

The tram has lifted us toward the sky.
Above us stand stark peaks of rock and ice;
Below us, well below the treeline, lie
Valleys calm and peaceful to our eyes.

Shielding faces against the wind's fierce bite,
We stand where no more trees and bushes grow
And marvel at the plants of dwarfish height
That huddle by a patch of remnant snow.

They hug the ground below the wind, dispatch
Their roots beneath the scree, and color every
Crag and crevice with their blooms. We catch
A glimpse of how determined life can be.

Here on these Alpine heights no winds that blow
Can devastate the flowers that want to grow.

Isobel Routly Stewart

Highway Interchange

the city dwindles in our mirror
and becomes a memory
we sip cocktails of blossoms
nibble the mountains
the road acrawl with city ants
trailing each other to the country
meeting a likewise thread
of country ants
escaping
to the city

Isobel Routly Stewart (b. 1917, Toronto, Canada) was published regularly during her late teens in *The Toronto Daily Star* and *The Globe and Mail* and republished in several Canadian monthlies. Since 1981, when she became an active writer again, she has won a number of awards and been published in *Amelia, The Formalist, Midwest Poetry Review, Odessa Review* and others. She appeared in Vols. 2, 3, and 4 of *The Poet's Domain*. She lives and writes in Woodbridge, VA.

Constance Tupper

Babushka

In the drab of Moscow's morning
She waits blank-eyed for the bus,
Her *avoska*—odd-chance bag—
Stringing empty from her arm,
Her dun stockings drooped, shoes
    run-over,
Hennaed hair scooped in a bun,
Stranding from her rose-print scarf.
In her thick fingers she holds,
Wrapped in yesterday's *Izvestia*,
A bunch of tumbling marigolds
Singing paeons to the sun.

Aunt Josie

Red-wigged, a valance of scallops
swagged across her brow,
Josie sat in the wicker rocker
that was home to her,
knitting down her days
like a ticking clock.
We knew her only prissy-prim,
the butt of children's jokes.

Married and deserted we were told,
Josie came home to sit
within the circle of contempt
called family charity,
passive in her lot
until one day she took her past
and tossed it from the upstairs window
with the contents of her chamber pot.

Constance Tupper (b. 1919, Manhattan, NY), an artist who has lived in Virginia for the past 30 years, is member of the Poetry Society of Virginia and has had poems published in *The Poet's Domain*, Vols. 2, 3, 4, and 5, and in *Orphic Lute*. In 1976 she won a Merit Award from *Woman's Day* magazine for her essay "Women, Today and Tomorrow."

Adrian Robert Unger

Where Are the Fairy Tales?

Innocence hides in the leisures of
    extreme,
Replaced by a vengeance
in a teenager's dream,
Plagued by resoundings—a fear of the
    day,
Locked up in files,
coerced to stay.
Sleeping Beauties now sleeping on
    vodka and pills;
Snow Whites on corners selling some
    thrills;
Cinderellas making movies in a
    backstreet garage;
Prince Charmings shooting-up to find a
    mirage.
Are these our fairy tales?
Do any remain?
Are the youths of today
The least bit sane?

Adrian Robert Unger (b. 1969, Alexandria, VA) is a student seeking his B.A. in English. He plans to teach creative writing at either the college or high-school level. He resides in Frederick, MD, where he is working on a collection of short stories and modernized fairy tales.

Evelyn Amuedo Wade

Two of a Kind—My Cat and Me

Angela deplores my vacuum cleaner.
"Monstrous contraption," she sniffs,
   "the work
of the devil, no less." An old lady,
suspicious of things beyond her control,
she eyes me warily, lips pursed together,
skirts the edges of the room
before escaping to the safety
of the basement, a basketful of
clean laundry, her refuge from the noise.

Shortly she is back when the racket
has subsided. Her nature is not a
   grudging one.
With only a touch of arrogance,
she approaches me, butts her face
   against
my hands, strokes my fingers with
her whiskers, picks daintily
at my knuckles with her teeth.

Within minutes, she sleeps on my lap,
quietly kneading my thighs,
purring her forgiveness.

I deplore the thunder storm.
Like, Angela, I too attribute the noise
to the devil, shrinking at the unholy
   clatter
that bellows in my ears,
cancels our picnic, pours pillows
of rain against my windows.

Mine is not a grudging nature
either. Shortly I am reconciled,
refrigerate the stuffed eggs, serve us
the tuna for lunch, and, like my cat,
offer my forgiveness to God.

Evelyn Amuedo Wade (b. , New Orleans, LA) holds degrees from American and George Washington Universities. She has lived in Virginia for forty-six years and has published hundreds of pieces in dozens of publications in this country and in Great Britain and taken many national awards for her poetry and her fiction. Professor Emeritus in the Virginia Community College System, she has two published books of poetry and a children's book, as well as another children's book scheduled for release in 1992.

Susannah A. Warner

Henbit and Winter Wheat

February—Will winter never end?
The gray dreariness drags at my spirits.
Even the pine trees are dark,
Their damp trunks black against the
    drab woods.
Suddenly I'm jolted out of the doldrums.
Bright emerald green,
Like the land of Oz,
The winter wheat speaks of spring to
    come.

March—Everyone looks for signs.
I simply watch the wheat field.
But today my field is a sea of purple.
I stop to look more closely.
Each bloom tiny, the henbit forms a
    solid blanket of color.
Let others look for the daffodils and
    robins.
Winter wheat and henbit say spring to
    me.
And when an occasional purple speck
    appears in my summer lawn,
I smile.

Susannah A. Warner (b. 1949, Norfolk, VA) a mathematics major who earned her M.A. degree from the College of William and Mary, makes her poetry debut in this edition. A computer scientist at NASA's Wallops Flight Facility, she lives in Onancock, VA.

Sharon Weinstein

Daughter's Breaks

Two weeks into high school basketball
my daughter broke her collar bone
roughhousing at her boyfriend's
who later bought her roses
with baby breath.

She didn't know the game,
The coach said "I'll teach you"
She learned fast
(daughters do)
and soon she could break
with the best of them
moving her body
to the rhythm of the ball
forgetting to eye the stands

It reminds me of the day
when she told me, in the car,
on the way to school,
before she learned to drive
and I was at the wheel;
"I hate you.
I've hated you
since I was ten years old."

And that reminds me
of the letter I sent
to my mother, yesterday
I told her that we both had beautiful
    eyes

Spring

Oh, that I would put my hands
on the warm skin
of men
And their eyes would light up
with joy

Sharon Weinstein (b. 1943, Detroit, MI) has been a steady contributor to *The Poet's Domain*. Professor of English and foreign languages at Norfolk State University, she teaches creative writing, American Literature, and Women's Studies courses. Her poems, stories, scholarly essays, and newspaper book reviews have appeared in such publications as *Western Humanities Review*, *Black Studies*, *Aethlon: The Journal of Sport Literature*, the *National Jewish Post & Opinion*, and *Lilith*. She has been a professor at The Center for the Humanities at Arizona State University and held an endowed chair (University Professor) at Hampton University.

Sharon Weinstein

Men Touching

They don't,
much.

And when they do,
it's so careful—
so very light,
as if the sensation
of hand against hand
cheek against cheek
creates a pressure
too dear
to bear

Sabbath Morning

The sunlight warm
The bird warbling
Infinitely sweet
I lay in his bed
after love
My heart humming.

In synagogue, later
We sing Hebrew songs
with the congregation

Making love, again.

Dying

He is a poem,
Lying there,
White,
Almost fetal;
A sleep so deep,
he can almost
not be roused.
Startled awake
he sees
with the gift
of the almost dead.
He shouts my name
Tells me I'm so
beautiful

Sharon Weinstein

Asks me to kiss him
I begin to cry
he says, "Kiss me,
Touch me."
I do.
"We were never
close," he murmurs.
"But I still love you,"
I protest.
"The details," he says,
dying, "the details,
we let them
get
in our way."

Katherine Roberts Wescott

Windjammer

Clipping along the coast of Maine
eleven to twelve knots
harp wind at our heels
exultant in silent speed
we never need the dory
except for nudging into harbor.
Whale-back Monhegan
indian Pemaquid
misty Isle Au Haut
we live the briny moment
with a fortune of full sail.
Red sky
sails furled
tucked in like the wings of gulls
we rock to sleep.
Sunrise finds our port hole under water
fish swimming by
ship listing
crew running cat-like at command.
Heave!
Hoist to ride the crest—
our captain and Columbus.

La! That was thirty years ago
yet lifts me up from my Virginia rocker
flinging arms and legs
against the morning's gale
to test my well-worn rigging.

Katherine Roberts Wescott (b. 1916, Nassawadox, VA) a major in art and primary education at Longwood College, is author and illustrator of two collections of poetry, *Salt and Sand* and *Untie the Ribbons*. Her poems have appeared in several anthologies including Vols. 2 and 3 of *The Poet's Domain*. She writes and paints from life in Onancock on her native Eastern Shore of Virginia.

Katherine Roberts Wescott

Really-rilly

Say what shall I wear—
      tilly lace,
      pink-a-dilly?
Don't cock an eyebrow
      I've a yen
      to be frilly.
Ice cream for breakfast
      or French eggs
      on my chili,
I'll waltz in the rain
      for I feel
      willy-nilly.
Joyous combustion
      I will sing
      tra-la-trilly.
Stop looking sideways;
      I've a right
      to be silly!

Moraeg E. Wood

Thought

A seed within my mind
Whirls and eddies constantly.
It moves too fast for me to grasp,
To fix in place with words.
Perhaps one day the seed may root
And, reaching for the sun, may bloom.
Then I shall have a flower to offer you.

Moraeg E. Wood (b. 1914, Jamaica, NY) moved to Charlottesville, VA, in 1986. She is a Foster Grandmother for two first-grade classes, where she, of course, promotes poetry. She won the Grand Prize in the Crossroads Contest in 1981 and has had poems published in a number of publications, including *The Connecticut River Review* and *Turtle Magazine*.

Deborah Woodward

Chase

Into the day,
wet, puddled, sweet,
he comes chasing
a playful breeze.

Arms outstretched,
he reaches, tender, green,
toward trees and feels
the stir of life, alike, new;
the wind and he each
sprig and cloud and wing embrace.

And he races full tilt,
whispering to himself and the wind
in secret joy, the chant of
boy and earth and sky.

Deborah Woodward (b. 1950, Cleveland, OH), writer and dancer, makes her poetry debut in this edition. She lives in Richmond, VA, where she is writing a children's book and a work of non-fiction.

Dorothy Yeatman

Classic Courtship

We come to each other as archaeologists
    to the dig,
Layer by layer unearthing fragments of
    old
Loves (known, missed, even dreamed).
Stare hard: this shard is glazed, charred
    by fire,
That fingertip fragment serrated by
    explosion,
This slice of pot still greenware never
    kilned.

Occasionally, we speak of coinage, gods.
Power succumbed to (why and when).
We piece together old journals, sacred
    texts,
Remember politics and taxes.

But dig before trying to stake common
    ground.
Say that the effort will be worth the
    broken nails,
The tattered hem, the jagged
    pick-picking
At our skulls, offering dead proof of
    good intent,
Attempts to form the perfect vessel,
    lasting love,
Which we are sure has never been
    done—
And may now never be done in such
    wreckage.

Dorothy Yeatman (b. 1948, Salisbury, MD), teaches English, theatre, and creative writing at Parkside High School in Salisbury, MD. Published since 1972, she has studied with poet Michael Waters, and dedicates most of her work to her parents.

Dorothy Yeatman

One Poet's Passions
(on the occasion of his fourth divorce)

It is a true error to marry with poets or to be by them.
John Berryman

Poets can love the unloveliest eyes,
Kiss even twisted lips. To explore fresh
Flesh is to savor exotic delicacy.

Tongues nurse the sweet and sweat,
Heavy with musky nectar, retreating
Like bees, filing flavors in hives

Of the mind. Each touch excites like
Cells. Giving and receiving blur as he
Becomes her body, caressing, soothing,

Arching into warm palms waiting
To be filled with further heat, smoothing
Rigid muscles into flowing energy

Shared, multiplied by two until the brain
Stops in sudden splendor, expanded
Past its own body into vistas

Where peace ordains release,
Seeding stars and sands with passion,
So that even beasts are blessed.

Poets can then rise to love the loveliest
Eyes, kiss pillowing lips. With this much
True, should he be faithful, too?

Dorothy Yeatman

Tidewater

Every other mile seems marked by a church—
Pentecostal, Evangelical, Wesleyan,
As if residents were always too cantankerous
And so kept to small congregations.

Generations, from Bestpitch to Taylor's to Blackwater,
Entered white clapboard houses lifting wooden crosses,
Open all weekend to welcome the hopeful
And the hopeless—all dressed to impress.

Frozen in wooden pews like crows on a wire—
Men in meeting suits they'd likely be buried in,
Women in housedresses ennobled by glittery brooches,
Children in too-tight collars and hand-me-downs
Come to the Rock to hear of the Lamb.

The hard shell Baptists don't sing, but declaim
"The Changing Year"—turning vowels to moans and croons.
Methodists praise psalmody, but amplified
To a multi-decibel din of "Activity and Zeal."

As if living in houses that become islands,
In a land made archipelago at the tide's whim,
Is only bearable if there is a fellow Fisherman,
Eternally vigilant, ready to reel us in.

Israel Zoberman

At Maidanek

Where shall I find you,
family of mine?
I've come to reclaim what
was left behind.
Perhaps someone can tell me
for I fail to see.
Only a blowing wind responds
to my plea.
The words of the Kaddish
I've brought to intone.
They too in the cold
air are lost.

I Longingly

I longingly crawled
into bed
to seek relief in night's
warm covers,
to protect against
day's nakedness.

There is a Sadness

There is a sadness that
is joy's gateway
and there is one
that merely perpetuates
itself.

Israel Zoberman (b. 1945, Chu, Kasakhastan, USSR), ordained as a reform rabbi by the Hebrew Union College—Jewish Institute of Religion in 1974, has been rabbi to Congregation Beth Chaverim in Virginia Beach since 1985. He studied at the University of Illinois and McCormick Theological Seminary (the only rabbi to receive a Doctor of Ministry in Pastoral Care and Counseling from this Presbyterian institution). His poetry and his translations from Hebrew have been published in *CCAR Journal*, the *Jewish Spectator*, the *American Rabbi*, *Moment*, and *The Poet's Domain*, Vol. 5.

INDEX OF AUTHORS

Barbara H. Achilles, Vienna, Va., 1-3
Patricia Adler, Woodbridge, Va., 4
M. Ray Allen, Clifton Forge, Va., 5
Joseph Awad, Richmond, Va., 7-8
Lolete Falck Barlow, Camp Springs, Md., 9
Mary Kay Belter, Vienna, Va., 10-11
Patsy Anne Bickerstaff, Weyers Cave, Va., 12-13
Sheila Cardano, Cape Charles, Va., 14
Kathy L. Cawthon, Hampton, Va., 15
Eunice de Chazeau, Alexandria, Va., 16-17
J.P.Q. El-Fayoumy, Virginia Beach, Va., 18
Laddie Fisher, Roanoke, Va., 19
Linda Beth Fristoe, Front Royal, Va., 20-22
Gertrude Gunther, Onancock, Va., 23-24
Ann Hawes, Alexandria, Va., 25
Barbara McKay Hewin, Williamsburg, Va., 26
Alana Maubury Hunter, Arlington, Va., 27
Agnes Nasmith Johnston, Alexandria, Va., 28-29
Carrie Jackson Karegeannes, Annandale, Va., 30
Jean P. Klotzbach, Columbia, Md., 31
Olive S. Lanham, Daytona Beach, Fla., 32
Mary Antil Lederman, Charlottesville, Va., 33-34
John Long, Richmond, Va., 35-37
Michael Hugh Lythgoe, Gainesville, Va., 38-40
Barbara Mabe, Wake, Va., 41
Joan Maloof, Quantico, Md., 42
Dorothy W. Millner, Alexandria, Va., 43
Medea E. Minnich, Ijamsville, Md., 44
Robert R. Montgomery, Hartfield, Va., 45
Geneva Ingraham Nasworthy, Woodstock, Va., 46
Julie Vakos Nordstrom, Exmore, Va., 48
Daisy Oblinger, Madison Heights, Va., 49
David J. Partie, Lynchburg, Va., 50-51
Jennifer Peachey, Bristol, Va., 52
Richard Raymond, III, Midlothian, Va., 53
Evelyn Ritchie, Richmond, Va., 54-56
Ada G. Sanderson, Falls Church, Va., 57
Askold Skalsky, Ijamsville, Md., 58
Barbara Smith, Newport News, Va., 59
Bruce Souders, Winchester, Va., 60-61
Isobel Routly Stewart, Woodbridge, Va., 62
Constance Tupper, Charlottesville, Va., 63

Adrian Robert Unger, Radford, Va., 64
Evelyn Amuedo Wade, Alexandria, Va., 65
Susannah A. Warner, Onancock, Va., 66
Sharon Weinstein, Virginia Beach, Va., 67-69
Katherine Roberts Wescott, Onancock, Va., 70-71
Moraeg E. Wood, Charlottesville, Va., 72
Deborah Woodward, Richmond, Va., 73
Dorothy Yeatman, Salisbury, Md., 74-76
Israel Zoberman, Virginia Beach, Va., 77